STEAM IN THE KITCHEN

CREATING
IN THE KITCHEN

THEIA LAKE

Published in 2024 by The Rosen Publishing Group, Inc.
2544 Clinton Street, Buffalo, NY 14224

Copyright © 2024 by The Rosen Publishing Group, Inc.

All rights reserved. No part of this book may be reproduced in any form without permission in writing from the publisher, except by a reviewer.

First Edition

Editor: Theresa Emminizer
Book Design: Rachel Rising

Photo Credits: Cover, p.1 Lordn/Shutterstock.com; pp. 4,6,8,10,12,14,16,18,20 porcelaniq/Shutterstock.com; p. 5 stockfour/Shutterstock.com; p. 7 Maksim Shmeljov/Shutterstock.com; pp. 9, 21 Prostock-studio/Shutterstock.com; p. 11 Viktar Malyshchyts/Shutterstock.com; p. 13 Alina Kruk/Shutterstock.com; p. 15 Anastasia_Panait/Shutterstock.com; p. 15 kuvona/Shutterstock.com; p. 17 Sea Wave/Shutterstock.com; p. 19 Iryna Dincer/Shutterstock.com.

Library of Congress Cataloging-in-Publication Data
Names: Lake, Theia, author.
Title: Creating in the kitchen / Theia Lake.
Description: Buffalo, New York : PowerKids Press, [2024] | Series: Steam in the kitchen | Includes bibliographical references (page 23) and index. | Audience: Grades K-1
Identifiers: LCCN 2023032108 (print) | LCCN 2023032109 (ebook) | ISBN 9781499443677 (library binding) | ISBN 9781499443660 (paperback) | ISBN 9781499443684 (ebook)
Subjects: LCSH: Cooking-Juvenile literature. | LCGFT: Cookbooks.
Classification: LCC TX652.5 .L344 2024 (print) | LCC TX652.5 (ebook) | DDC 641.5-dc23/eng/20230724
LC record available at https://lccn.loc.gov/2023032108
LC ebook record available at https://lccn.loc.gov/2023032109

Manufactured in the United States of America

Some of the images in this book illustrate individuals who are models. The depictions do not imply actual situations or events.

CPSIA Compliance Information: Batch #CWPK24. For Further Information contact Rosen Publishing at 1-800-237-9932.

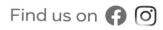

CONTENTS

Get Creative 4
Gather Your Ingredients 6
Find Your Flavor 8
Make a Rainbow 10
Food Face 12
Crafty Critters 14
Cook It Up! 16
Mix, Bake, Create 18
You're a Chef! 20
Glossary 22
For More Information 23
Index 24

Get Creative

The kitchen is a great place to get **creative**. You can make almost anything! Just use your **imagination**. You could invent a new dish. Or find a new way to make an old favorite. Cooking food is a fun, hands-on way of practicing creativity. It's tasty too!

Gather Your Ingredients

Ask your caregiver to help you pick out foods to **experiment** with. Look in the cupboards and fridge. Gather your **ingredients** and place them on a table. Be sure to practice food safety. Never handle raw (uncooked) meat or seafood without help from a grown-up.

Find Your Flavor

Once you've gathered your ingredients, take a moment to look at them. Think about what you'd like your dish to taste like. Should it be sweet or salty? Maybe you want to make a whole new flavor, or taste, that's a little bit of both!

Make a Rainbow

Start crafting your dish. What do you want your food to look like? Try making a rainbow! Group your foods together by color and shape them in an **arc**. Here are some ideas:

- **red:** strawberries
- **orange:** oranges
- **yellow:** bananas
- **green:** cucumbers
- **blue:** blueberries
- **purple:** grapes

Food Face

Try making a food face outline! Ask a grown-up to help you cut up fruits, veggies, or pieces of cheese. Have fun arranging, or placing, them however you like! Here are a few ideas to get you started:

- **hair:** broccoli
- **eyes:** cucumbers
- **nose:** pepper
- **face:** green beans
- **ears:** sliced cucumbers

13

Crafty Critters

Why not craft some tasty critters? You could turn a sliced apple into a crab! Or make a lion out of oranges, bananas, and berries. Play around with the different shapes and colors of your ingredients and see what animals you come up with!

Cook It Up!

Some of your ingredients may need to be cooked. Rice and pasta are great bases to make meals with. And they come in lots of fun shapes, sizes, and colors! Ask a grown-up to help you **boil** water to cook your pasta or rice.

Mix, Bake, Create

There are millions of ways to put together flour, milk, eggs, sugar, and butter to turn them into something tasty. Try baking! Experiment with new cookie or muffin **recipes**. Just always make sure a grown-up helps you with the oven. And never eat raw batter or **dough**.

You're a Chef!

With a few ingredients, a little help, and a great imagination, you can make anything you want! Take pictures of the food you make. Write down your favorite recipes and make them into your own cookbook! There are so many ways to create in the kitchen.

GLOSSARY

arc: A shape or line that is curved and similar to part of a circle.

boil: To make a liquid so hot that bubbles are formed and rise to the top.

creative: Showing or having the skill of coming up with new ideas or making new creations.

dough: A mixture of mainly flour or meal and a liquid that is able to be rolled or kneaded.

experiment: A scientific test in which you carry out a series of actions and watch what happens in order to learn about something.

imagination: The power of the mind to come up with new ideas.

ingredient: A food that is mixed with other foods.

recipe: An explanation of how to make food.

FOR MORE INFORMATION

BOOKS

Food Network. *The Recipe-a-Day Kids Cookbook.* New York, NY: Hearst Home Kids, 2022.

Williams, Morgan. *Careers for People Who Love Cooking.* New York, NY: Rosen Publishing, 2021.

WEBSITES

America's Test Kitchen
www.americastestkitchen.com/kids
Find fun recipes to make with your family!

Science Buddies
www.sciencebuddies.org/stem-activities/ice-cream-bag
Learn how to make ice cream in a bag!

Publisher's note to educators and parents: Our editors have carefully reviewed these websites to ensure that they are suitable for students. Many websites change frequently, however, and we cannot guarantee that a site's future contents will continue to meet our high standards of quality and educational value. Be advised that students should be closely supervised whenever they access the internet.

INDEX

A
animals, 14
apple, 14

B
baking, 18
bananas, 10, 14
berries, 10, 14

C
color, 10, 14, 16
cucumbers, 10, 12

F
food safety, 6

P
pasta, 16

R
rice, 16

S
shape, 10, 14, 16